Machines on the Farm

by Teddy Borth

ABDO
ON THE FARM
Kids

www.abdopublishing.com

Published by Abdo Kids, a division of ABDO, PO Box 398166, Minneapolis, Minnesota 55439.

Copyright © 2015 by Abdo Consulting Group, Inc. International copyrights reserved in all countries. No part of this book may be reproduced in any form without written permission from the publisher.

Printed in the United States of America, North Mankato, Minnesota.

052014

092014

 THIS BOOK CONTAINS RECYCLED MATERIALS

Photo Credits: Shutterstock, Thinkstock, © DeshaCAM p.9 / Shutterstock.com

Production Contributors: Teddy Borth, Jennie Forsberg, Grace Hansen

Design Contributors: Candice Keimig, Laura Rask, Dorothy Toth

Library of Congress Control Number: 2013952565

Cataloging-in-Publication Data

Borth, Teddy.

 Machines on the farm / Teddy Borth.

   p. cm. -- (On the farm)

ISBN 978-1-62970-054-0 (lib. bdg.)

Includes bibliographical references and index.

1. Agricultural machinery--Juvenile literature.   I. Title.

631.3--dc23

                    2013952565

Table of Contents

Machines on the Farm

Many machines are used on the farm. Machines help farmers do chores.

Tractor

Tractors pull things. Tractors are part of most jobs.

7

Cultivator

Cultivators get soil ready for seeds. They loosen the ground. They also remove **weeds**.

9

Planter

Planters plant seeds in rows.

These seeds grow into crops.

Sprayer

Sprayers give plants water. They have long arms to reach many plants.

Sprinkler

Sprinklers are on long pipes. They usually move in a circle **pattern**.

14

Combine

Combines **harvest** grain.
They cut the grain. Straw
is left behind.

16

Hay Rake

Hay rakes put hay and straw into rows. The rows make it easier to pick up.

19

Baler

Balers clear the field. They press cut hay and straw into bales. The bales are round or rectangular.

More Facts

- The word tractor comes from Latin and means "to pull."

- There is a **competition** for tractor pulling. The winner is the person whose tractor can pull the weighted sled the farthest.

- Some balers can make bales that weigh over a ton (907.2 kg).

- The largest planter in the world can plant seeds in 48 rows at once!

Glossary

competition – an event or contest in which people compete.

harvest – what is gathered from ripe crops.
A harvest may be vegetables, fruits, or grains.

pattern – regular, repeated movement.

weed – a wild, unwanted plant.

Index

abdokids.com

Use this code to log on to abdokids.com and access crafts, games, videos and more!

Abdo Kids Code:
OMK0540